Make light work of Year 1 English with CGP

Grappling with all the skills pupils need for Year 1 English is no walk in the park — the secret is heaps of regular practice.

And if it's practice you're looking for, this CGP book is jam-packed with it! It's bursting with skills from the Year 1 curriculum, with an activity for every day of summer term.

But hold your horses! We've also included helpful examples and bright pictures to keep pupils engaged. Use this book at home or in class...anywhere you want, really!

What CGP is all about

Our sole aim here at CGP is to produce the highest quality books — carefully written, immaculately presented and dangerously close to being funny.

Then we work our socks off to get them out to you — at the cheapest possible prices.

Contents

☑ Use the tick boxes to help keep a record of which tests have been attempted.

Week 1

☑ Day 1 1
☑ Day 2 2
☑ Day 3 3
☑ Day 4 4
☑ Day 5 5

Week 2

☑ Day 1 6
☑ Day 2 7
☑ Day 3 8
☑ Day 4 9
☑ Day 5 10

Week 3

☑ Day 1 11
☑ Day 2 12
☑ Day 3 13
☑ Day 4 14
☑ Day 5 15

Week 4

☑ Day 1 16
☑ Day 2 17
☑ Day 3 18
☑ Day 4 19
☑ Day 5 20

Week 5

☑ Day 1 21
☑ Day 2 22
☑ Day 3 23
☑ Day 4 24
☑ Day 5 25

Week 6

☑ Day 1 26
☑ Day 2 27
☑ Day 3 28
☑ Day 4 29
☑ Day 5 30

Week 7

☑ Day 1 31
☑ Day 2 32
☑ Day 3 33
☑ Day 4 34
☑ Day 5 35

Week 8

☑ Day 1 36
☑ Day 2 37
☑ Day 3 38
☑ Day 4 39
☑ Day 5 40

Week 9

☑ Day 1 41
☑ Day 2 42
☑ Day 3 43
☑ Day 4 44
☑ Day 5 45

Week 10

☑ Day 1 46
☑ Day 2 47
☑ Day 3 48
☑ Day 4 49
☑ Day 5 50

Week 11

☑ Day 1 51
☑ Day 2 52
☑ Day 3 53
☑ Day 4 54
☑ Day 5 55

Week 12

☑ Day 1 56
☑ Day 2 57
☑ Day 3 58
☑ Day 4 59
☑ Day 5 60

Answers 61

Published by CGP

ISBN: 978 1 78908 677 5

Editors: Emma Cleasby, Alex Fairer, Rebecca Greaves, Catherine Heygate, Becca Lakin, Katya Parkes

With thanks to Claire Boulter and Juliette Green for the proofreading.

With thanks to Lottie Edwards for the copyright research.

Cover and Graphics used throughout the book © www.edu-clips.com

Printed by Elanders Ltd, Newcastle upon Tyne.
Based on the classic CGP style created by Richard Parsons.

How to Use this Book

- This book contains <u>60 pages of daily English practice</u>.

- We've split them into <u>12 sections</u> — that's roughly one for <u>each week</u> of the Year 1 <u>Summer term</u>.

- Each week is made up of <u>5 pages</u>, so there's one for <u>every school day</u> of the term (Monday – Friday).

- Each page should take about <u>10 minutes</u> to complete.

- The pages contain a <u>mix</u> of topics from <u>Year 1</u> English. <u>New Year 1 topics</u> are gradually introduced as you go through the book.

- The pages <u>increase in difficulty</u> as you progress through the book.

- <u>Answers</u> can be found at the <u>back</u> of the book.

- Each page looks something like this:

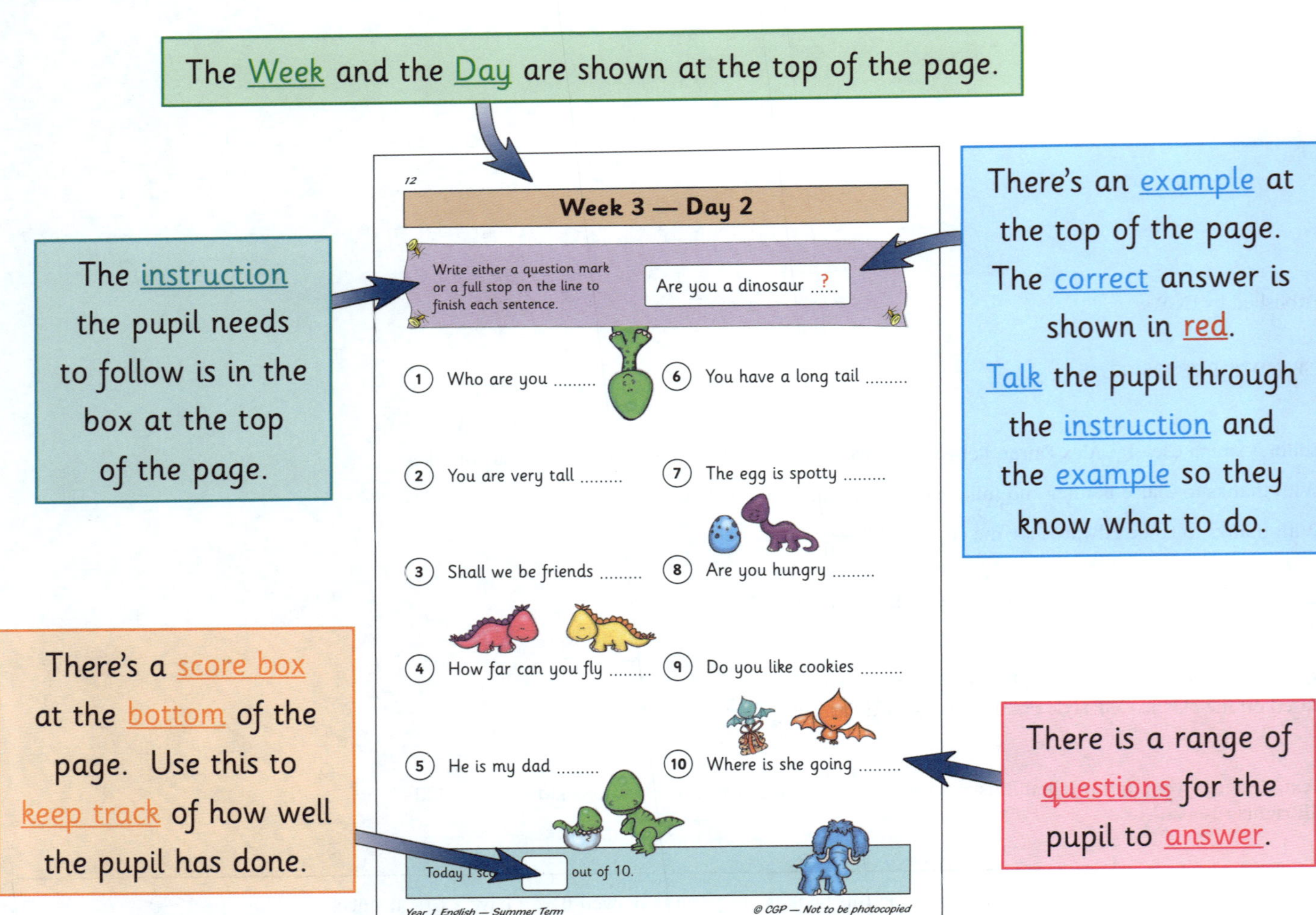

Week 1 — Day 1

Write the words in the correct order to make a sentence. Then add a full stop to the sentence.

| a | had | We | race |

We had a race.

1 | the | is | winner | He |

....

2 | running | I | races | like |

....

3 | Ben | very | fast | ran |

....

4 | has | medal | Oti | a |

....

Today I scored ☐ out of 8.

     Year 1 English — Summer Term

Week 1 — Day 2

Rearrange the letters in the box to make a word that fits in the sentence. Write the word on the line.

We swam to a ...*cave*...

c v a e

---

(1) I .... into the sea.

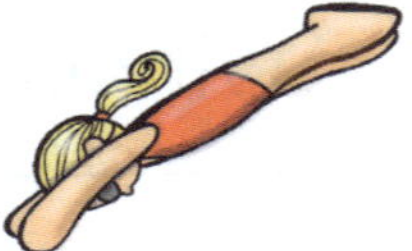

v d i e

(2) He surfed a big ....

w v a e

(3) They .... the water.

o v e l

(4) I .... so much fun.

e h a v

(5) She saw .... fish.

f i e v

(6) Mum .... me a lolly.

a g v e

Today I scored [ ] out of 6.

Week 1 — Day 3

Read the sentences. Add full stops where they are needed.

I am six years old. It was my birthday yesterday.

1) I had a party All my friends were there

2) We all wore fancy dress Everyone looked good

3) I wore my monster costume It is blue

4) Tia came as a bee She loves insects

5) Dad made a cake He put candles on top

6) We played games Pass the parcel is the best

Today I scored [   ] out of 12.

Year 1 English — Summer Term

Week 1 — Day 4

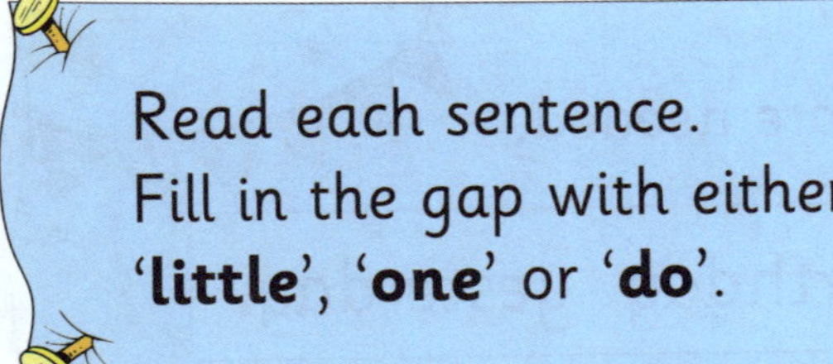

.....Do.... you like to dance?

1 Will you .... a dance with me?

2 I can show you what to ....

3 First take .... big jump forward.

4 Then do a .... hop to the right.

5 March on the spot a .... bit.

6 Kick .... of your legs in the air.

7 Now .... it all again!

Today I scored [ ] out of 7.

Week 1 — Day 5

Read the text, then answer the questions.

1) What kind of text is this? Tick one box.

a list ☐   a story ☐   a poem ☐

2) How many tents do they need to bring?

3) Where do you think they are going? Circle one box.

camping	swimming	to the zoo

4) What kind of food is not in the text? Circle one thing.

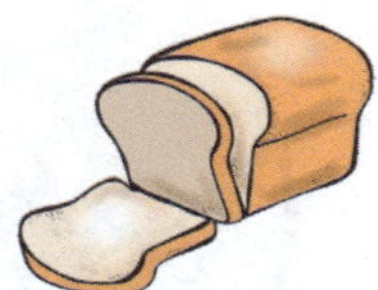   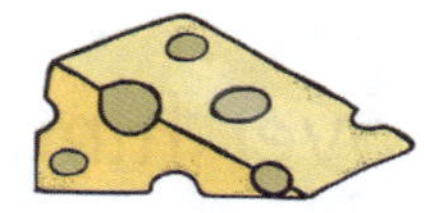      

Today I scored ☐ out of 4.

Year 1 English — Summer Term

Week 2 — Day 1

Read each sentence. Circle the correct spelling of the word in bold.

1. Bella is **prowd** / **proud** of her plant.

2. **How** / **Hou** many leaves does it have?

3. Nigel plants seeds in the **ground** / **grownd**.

4. The mud is **broun** / **brown** and sticky.

5. Emma **found** / **fownd** a huge leaf.

6. She is **alloued** / **allowed** to keep it.

7. Eric put his arms **arownd** / **around** the tree.

8. The tree **towers** / **touers** over him.

Today I scored ☐ out of 8.

Week 2 — Day 2

Join each pair of sentences together using '**and**'.
Write out the new sentence.

I have a cat. His name is Leo.

I have a cat and his name is Leo.

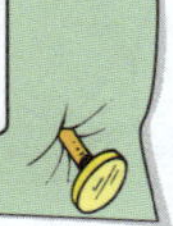

1 Her cat is grey. Yours is black.

....

....

2 My cat was playing. She got wet.

....

....

3 Tiger was tired. He fell asleep.

....

....

Today I scored ☐ out of 3.

Year 1 English — Summer Term

Week 2 — Day 3

Draw lines to join each sentence to the missing word.

I heard a lion _____. — roar

1) The zebra _____ when I tickle it.

2) The sloth will _____ on the branch.

3) The toucan sat on his _____.

4) The rhino has _____ skin.

5) The hippo has _____ in the mud.

6) The baby bears enjoy _____ each other.

7) The giraffe is _____ for her lunch.

rest

wrinkly

wriggles

wrestling

wrist

ready

rolled

Today I scored [ ] out of 7.

Week 2 — Day 4

Circle one word in each sentence that should have a capital letter.

1 Last week, i read five books.

2 Fen's book is set in bristol.

3 The best writer is amy Peterson.

4 Malia and I like books about japan.

5 I want to be a writer when i am older.

6 We go to the library every friday.

7 my sister likes reading about lorries.

Today I scored ☐ out of 7.

Year 1 English — Summer Term

Week 2 — Day 5

Read the poem, then answer the questions below.

I walk in the hills,	I hear the April **shouers**
What do I see?	Fall on the soggy ground.
Lots of yellow daffodils,	Raindrops sit on flowers
The branches of a tree.	That are growing all around.

1 What can I see on my walk? Circle two things.

2 What month is it in the poem? Tick one box.

January ☐   April ☐   September ☐

3 Write the correct spelling of the word in bold.

shouers ....

4 What sits on the flowers?

....

Today I scored ☐ out of 5.

Week 3 — Day 1

Read the sentences, then find the words in bold in the wordsearch. Circle the words when you find them.

1 We have to **stay** inside.

2 Maya draws a **snail**.

3 Fay **plays** with blocks.

4 Calvin **paints** a picture.

5 Eli finds **eight** pens.

6 They have a card **game**.

L	E	D	T	M	G	E	L	S	S	E	O
T	I	N	E	S	E	P	A	I	N	T	S
A	G	A	M	E	O	E	G	P	A	I	L
U	H	F	U	P	L	A	Y	S	I	C	B
S	T	A	Y	O	S	M	P	A	L	N	Y

Today I scored [ ] out of 6.

Year 1 English — Summer Term

Week 3 — Day 2

Write either a question mark or a full stop on the line to finish each sentence.

Are you a dinosaur ...**?**...

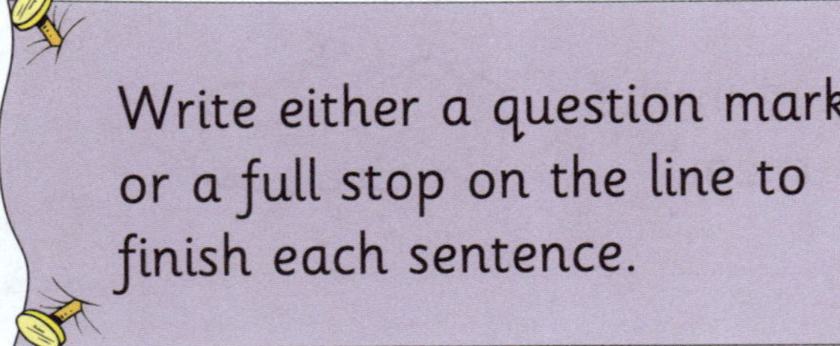

1 Who are you ....

6 You have a long tail ....

2 You are very tall ....

7 The egg is spotty ....

3 Shall we be friends ....

8 Are you hungry ....

4 How far can you fly ....

9 Do you like cookies ....

5 He is my dad ....

10 Where is she going ....

Today I scored ☐ out of 10.

Week 3 — Day 3

Read each sentence. Circle 'yes' or 'no' to show whether the sentence matches the picture.

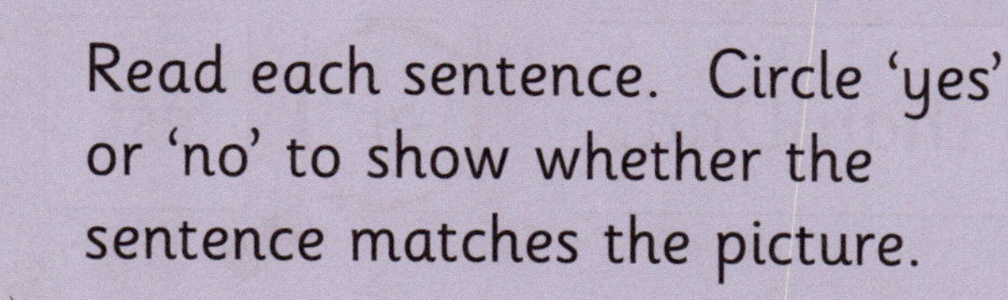

1 The fridge is open.

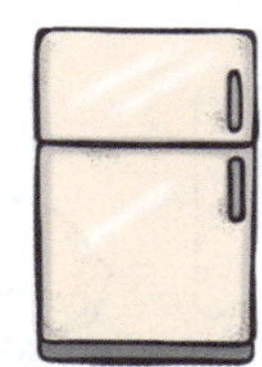

yes　no

2 Gemma enjoys her juice.

yes　no

3 The fudge is on a plate.

yes　no

4 Geri's jug is huge.

yes　no

5 Roger has a large orange.

yes　no

6 I have some jam for you.

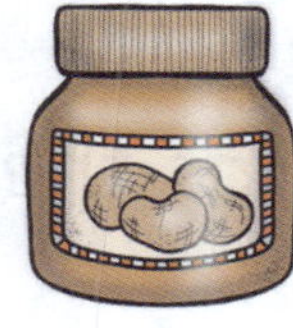

yes　no

7 Jenni eats some porridge.

yes　no

8 I spilt jelly on my jumper.

yes　no

Today I scored ☐ out of 8.

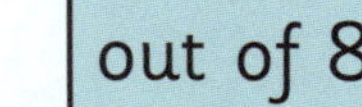

Year 1 English — Summer Term

Week 3 — Day 4

Read each sentence. Circle the correct ending to complete the word in bold.

He is **strict**___ than Dad.   (er)   est

1. My grandma is **old**___ than my grandpa.   er   est

2. You have the **long**___ hair of all.   er   est

3. I am **tall**___ than my sisters.   er   est

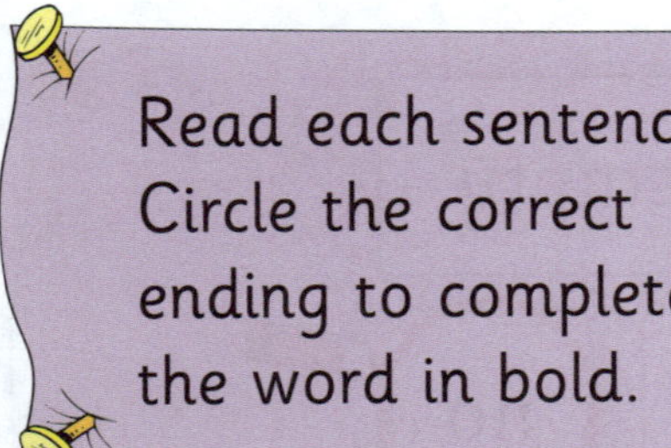

4. He has the **loud**___ voice out of us.   er   est

5. Nick is the **fast**___ in our class.   er   est

6. My brother is **young**___ than me.   er   est

7. Kelvin is **short**___ than Mia.   er   est

8. Dev is the **clever**___ out of everyone.   er   est

Today I scored ⬜ out of 8.

Week 3 — Day 5

Read the text, then answer the questions.

All About Unicorns

- Unicorns have large horns and silky **tayls**.
- They can jump higher than any other animal.
- Unicorns love porridge. They also like jelly.
- They are afraid of badgers, snails and jam.

1 Write the correct spelling of the word in bold.

tayls ....

2 What are unicorns good at? Circle one thing.

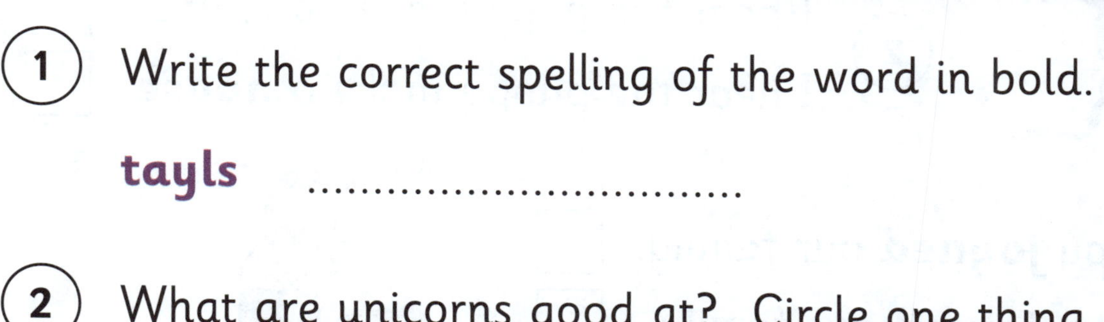

singing	jumping	painting

3 What do unicorns like to eat? Write down two things.

.... and ....

4 Draw a picture in the box showing one thing that unicorns are afraid of.

Today I scored [   ] out of 5.

Year 1 English — Summer Term

Week 4 — Day 1

Read each pair of sentences. Tick the sentence where the word in bold is spelt correctly.

The **boy** got a puppy. ✔
The **boi** got a puppy. ☐

1
Do not **spoyl** the surprise. ☐
Do not **spoil** the surprise. ☐

2
I hear the puppy make a **noise**. ☐
I hear the puppy make a **noyse**. ☐

3
The puppy **joyned** our family. ☐
The puppy **joined** our family. ☐

4
I will buy her some dog **tois**. ☐
I will buy her some dog **toys**. ☐

5
She will not **annoy** you. ☐
She will not **annoi** you. ☐

6
He **poynts** at the door. ☐
He **points** at the door. ☐

Today I scored ☐ out of 6.

Week 4 — Day 2

Circle '!' or '?' to show whether each sentence should end with an exclamation mark or a question mark.

Look at me  ! ?

(1) What a fast skater Jon is   !   ?

(2) How did you do that   !   ?

(3) He is standing on one leg   !   ?

(4) Can they do lots of tricks   !   ?

(5) Why did that girl fall over   !   ?

(6) How cosy your scarf looks   !   ?

(7) Do you think he is the best skater   !   ?

(8) Skating with my sister is fun   !   ?

Today I scored ☐ out of 8.

Year 1 English — Summer Term

Week 4 — Day 3

Add either 'f', 'ff' or 'ph' to the words in bold to complete the sentences.

I got a ra..ff..le ticket.

1 You can win lots of **di**...........**erent** things.

2 Bilal won some **flu**...........**y** earmuffs.

3 This teddy is so **so**...........**t**.

4 Fred just won a ....**ancy** pen.

5 I cuddled my new **ele**...........**ant** toy.

6 I wanted to win the box of **to**...........**ees**.

7 Can you take a ....**oto** of me with my prize?

Today I scored [ ] out of 7.

Week 4 — Day 4

Write the words in the correct order to make a sentence. Then add a full stop to the sentence.

squirrel | acorns | The | wants

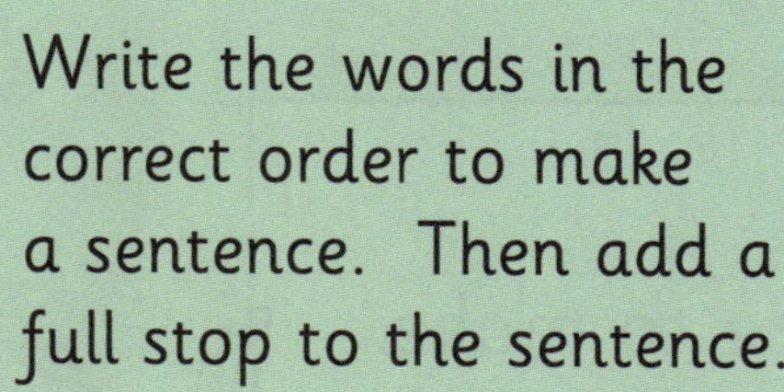

The squirrel wants acorns.

1 trees | He | in | the | searches

....

2 behind | the | looks | flowers | He

....

3 are | none | There | here | up

....

4 of | lots | acorns | He | finds

....

Today I scored [ ] out of 8.

Year 1 English — Summer Term

Week 4 — Day 5

Read the text, then answer the questions.

Freya's Great Climb

Freya was doing PE. She had a **choyce** to make.
Would she climb the ladder or stay on the ground?
Her class watched her as she decided. It made
her nervous. Finally, she started up the ladder.
Soon, she could almost touch the roof of the gym!

1 Write the correct spelling of the word in bold.

choyce ....

2 What is Freya climbing?

....

3 What did everybody do that made Freya nervous?

teased her ☐   made noise ☐   watched her ☐

4 Where is Freya? Circle one place.

Today I scored ☐ out of 4.

Week 5 — Day 1

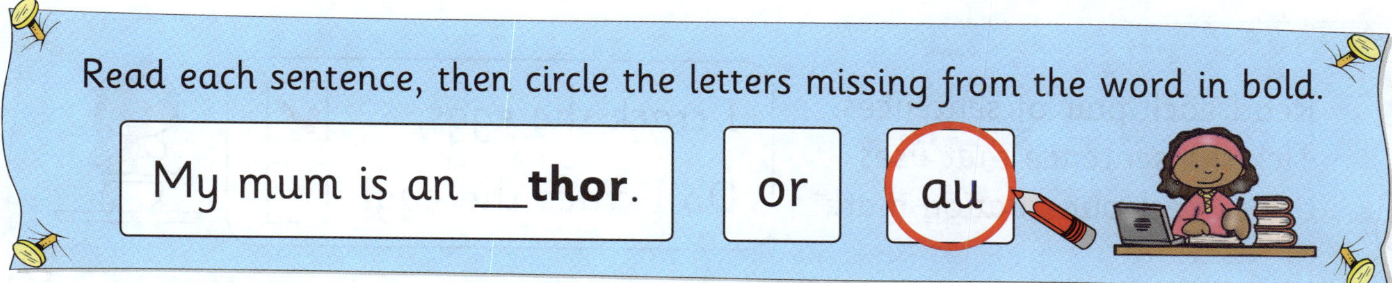

1 Mum does **m__** writing than me.
aw   ore

2 I **s__** her books in the shop.
or   aw

3 I like writing **st__ies** too.
or   our

4 I write them **f__** my sister.
aw   or

5 My new story is about a **h__nted** house.
au   ore

6 Spooky creatures **c__se** trouble.
aw   au

7 I will **dr__** a picture of it.
or   aw

Today I scored [ ] out of 7.

Year 1 English — Summer Term

Week 5 — Day 2

Read each pair of sentences. Tick the sentence that uses the correct punctuation mark.

> I crack the eggs. ✓
> Do I crack the egg! ☐

1 Why did you make such a mess. ☐
Stop making such a mess! ☐

2 You can weigh out the flour. ☐
How much flour do we need! ☐

3 Where is the big cake tin! ☐
We need to find a big cake tin. ☐

4 You must not touch the oven? ☐
Do not touch the oven! ☐

5 Now we add the strawberry icing. ☐
Should I add the strawberry icing! ☐

6 That is a large and fancy cake? ☐
What a large and fancy cake! ☐

Today I scored ☐ out of 6.

Week 5 — Day 3

1. It is ___ to walk around.

twice

2. I have been here ___ before.

nice

3. Where is the ___ fair?

spaces

4. It was hard to find parking ___.

science

5. People work in those ___.

cinema

6. We ___ our way through the crowd.

forced

7. I saw a film at that ___.

offices

Today I scored ☐ out of 7.

Year 1 English — Summer Term

Week 5 — Day 4

Use the letters in the boxes to complete the words. Then use the letters marked with pink dots to spell the final word.

f .o. o .t. b a .l. l

l	t
	o

1 l .... n ..... h ..... o x

	b
u	
c	

2 w h i .... e ..... o a ..... d

t	b
r	

3 c l ..... s .... r ..... o m

	a
o	s

4 p l a ..... g r o ..... n ....

u	y
d	

5 w o ..... k s .... e .... t

	h
r	
	e

6 I like to play o .... i ....

Today I scored [ ] out of 6.

Week 5 — Day 5

Read the poem, then answer the questions below.

> There has not been a bigger goose
> Than my dear old pet, Mr Bruce.
> When he was **bawn**, he was a normal size,
> But then we got a big surprise.
> If Mr Bruce grows a little more,
> Then we will need a new barn door!

1 What kind of animal is Mr Bruce?

....

2 Write the correct spelling of the word in bold.

bawn ....

3 What surprised the person in the poem about Mr Bruce?

He grew a lot. ☐   He was born. ☐   He was small. ☐

4 What will happen if Mr Bruce gets taller?

....

Today I scored ☐ out of 4.

   Year 1 English — Summer Term

Week 6 — Day 1

Read each sentence, then circle the word in bold that is spelt correctly.

(1) The **crue** / **crew** are on their way.

(2) They rescued a cat from the **rufe** / **roof**.

(3) They flashed their **blue** / **bloo** lights.

(4) I want to be a firefighter **too** / **tew**.

(5) I heard the sirens from my **rume** / **room**.

(6) The policewoman looked for a stolen **floot** / **flute**.

(7) He **floo** / **flew** over in a helicopter.

(8) It is **trew** / **true** that they are heroes.

Today I scored [ ] out of 8.

Week 6 — Day 2

Write the words in the correct order to make a sentence. Remember to add the punctuation mark in the correct place.

happened   morning   What   ?   this

What happened this morning?

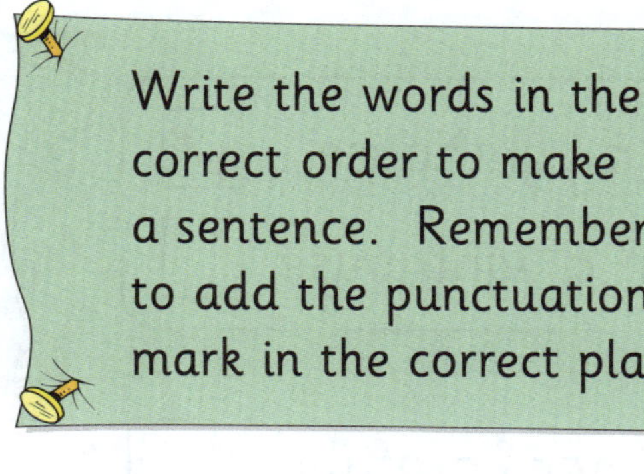

1   asks   She   .   questions   him

2   she   did   ?   What   say

3   camera   .   He   the   holds

4   the   nice   weather   ?   Is

Today I scored ☐ out of 4.

Year 1 English — Summer Term

Week 6 — Day 3

Read each pair of sentences. Tick the sentence where the word in bold is spelt correctly.

Ella **works** in a lighthouse. ✔
Ella **whorks** in a lighthouse. ☐

1. She **whatches** the weather carefully. ☐
   She **watches** the weather carefully. ☐

2. **Which** way is the ship sailing? ☐
   Wich way is the ship sailing? ☐

3. A light is coming from the **window**. ☐
   A light is coming from the **whindow**. ☐

4. The captain turns the **weel** to steer the ship. ☐
   The captain turns the **wheel** to steer the ship. ☐

5. It is **whindy** at the top of the lighthouse. ☐
   It is **windy** at the top of the lighthouse. ☐

6. Sometimes, Ella sees a **wale** in the sea. ☐
   Sometimes, Ella sees a **whale** in the sea. ☐

Today I scored ☐ out of 6.

Week 6 — Day 4

Add '**s**' or '**es**' to the words in bold to complete the sentences.

We found dinosaur **bone**.....s....

1 Haruki and Jack found two **skull**............

2 My camera is in one of the **box**...........

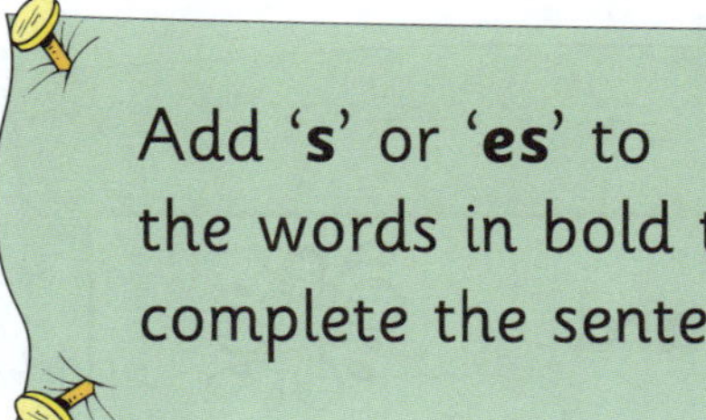

3 Those dinosaurs had large **head**..........!

4 She **brush**.......... all of the soil away.

5 Raina **put**.......... the small bones in jars.

6 Finn **touch**.......... the broken pieces.

7 Alice **want**.......... to find an old tooth.

8 Gino digs near the **bush**..........

Today I scored ☐ out of 8.

Year 1 English — Summer Term

Week 6 — Day 5

Read the text, then answer the questions.

Job Opening — Lifeguard

Do you want a new job? Then come and join our friendly lifeguard crew! Your job will **inclood**:

- watching the pool
- rescuing anyone who needs help
- stopping people running in case they slip

1 Write the correct spelling of the word in bold.

inclood ....

2 What do lifeguards have to do? Tick two boxes.

rescue people ☐   watch the pool ☐   chase people ☐

3 Why do lifeguards stop people running?

....

4 Rewrite this sentence so that it makes sense.

'**He silver his whistle blew.**'

....

Today I scored ☐ out of 5.

Week 7 — Day 1

Read each sentence.
Circle the correct spelling
of the word in bold.

Kit is a polar **bear** / **bair**.

1 Karl has a **spare** / **spair** sheet of paper.

2 Abby sits on her **chare** / **chair**.

3 Stephen likes to **wair** / **wear** warm hats.

4 Kayla has a **pair** / **pare** of red boots.

5 Tom **stares** / **stears** at the cake.

6 India has her foot in the **are** / **air**.

7 Eric always **shares** / **shairs** his presents.

8 Clara has gone to the **fair** / **fear**.

Today I scored ⬚ out of 8.

Year 1 English — Summer Term

Week 7 — Day 2

Write either a full stop or a question mark on each line to finish the sentence.

Can we climb the tree ...**?**....

1 Can you reach the top of the tree........

2 I am holding on as tight as I can........

3 Shelly is hanging upside down........

4 How did you get up there so fast........

5 There is a very good view from the top........

6 Are your arms feeling tired yet........

7 Which tree shall we go up next........

8 I will sit on this branch for a rest........

Today I scored ☐ out of 8.

Week 7 — Day 3

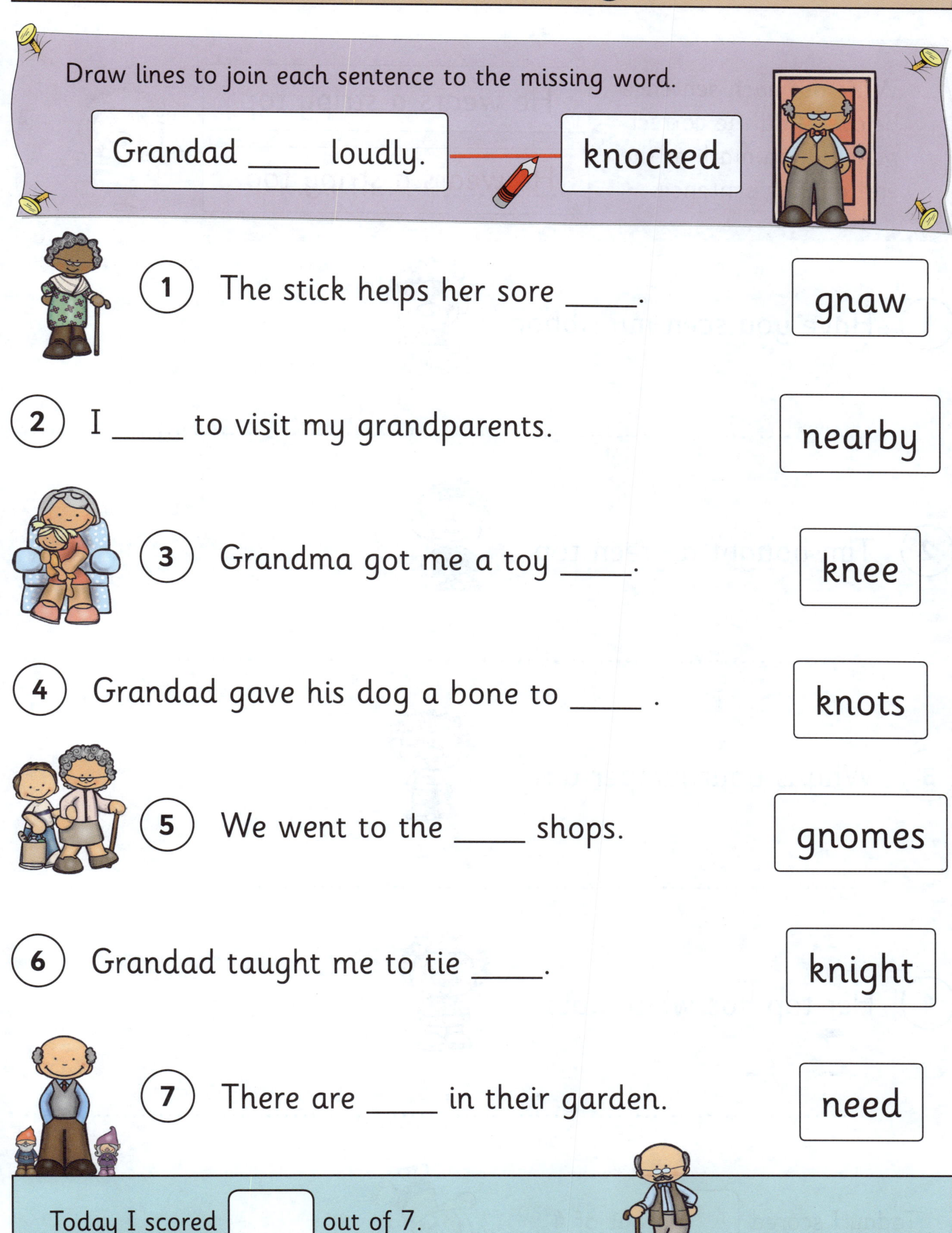

Draw lines to join each sentence to the missing word.

Grandad _____ loudly. —— knocked

1) The stick helps her sore _____.

gnaw

2) I _____ to visit my grandparents.

nearby

3) Grandma got me a toy _____.

knee

4) Grandad gave his dog a bone to _____ .

knots

5) We went to the _____ shops.

gnomes

6) Grandad taught me to tie _____.

knight

7) There are _____ in their garden.

need

Today I scored [ ] out of 7.

Year 1 English — Summer Term

Week 7 — Day 4

Write out each sentence below. Add the correct punctuation mark at the end of each sentence.

He wears a stripy top

He wears a stripy top.

1. Have you seen my ribbon

2. Tim bought a green top

3. Why is your jumper dirty

4. Her top has white dots

Today I scored ☐ out of 4.

Week 7 — Day 5

Read the text, then answer the questions.

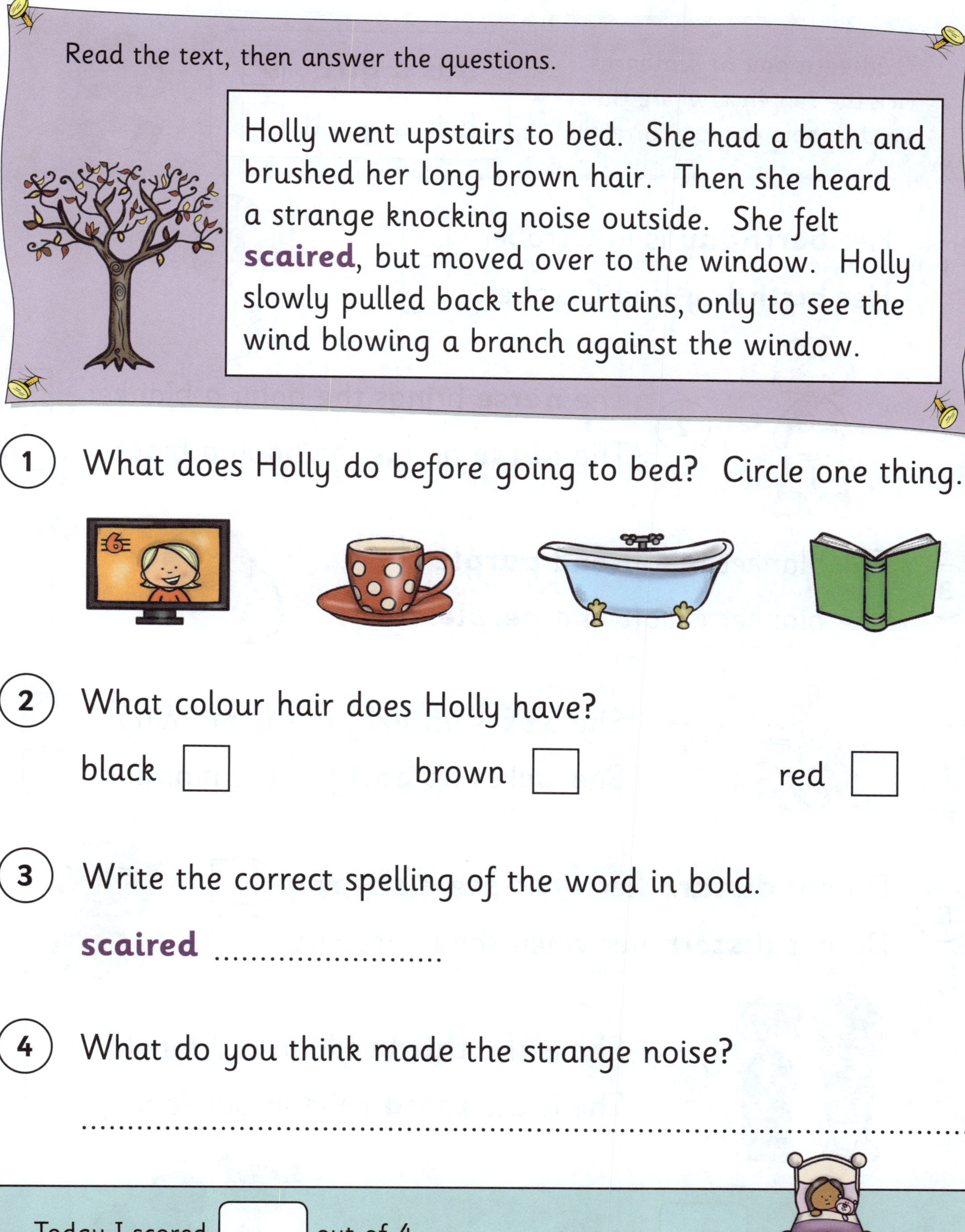

Holly went upstairs to bed. She had a bath and brushed her long brown hair. Then she heard a strange knocking noise outside. She felt **scaired**, but moved over to the window. Holly slowly pulled back the curtains, only to see the wind blowing a branch against the window.

1 What does Holly do before going to bed? Circle one thing.

2 What colour hair does Holly have?

black ☐   brown ☐   red ☐

3 Write the correct spelling of the word in bold.

scaired ....

4 What do you think made the strange noise?

....

Today I scored ☐ out of 4.

     Year 1 English — Summer Term

Week 8 — Day 1

Read each pair of sentences. Tick the sentence where the word in bold is spelt correctly.

It is a **girl**! ✔
It is a **gurl**! ☐

1
Her **berthday** is in October. ☐
Her **birthday** is in October. ☐

2
The **nerse** brings the baby a blanket. ☐
The **nurse** brings the baby a blanket. ☐

3
The blanket is soft and **purple**. ☐
The blanket is soft and **perple**. ☐

4
She wakes up **urly** in the morning. ☐
She wakes up **early** in the morning. ☐

5
Do not **disturb** her when she is sleeping. ☐
Do not **disterb** her when she is sleeping. ☐

6
She is the **third** child in our family. ☐
She is the **therd** child in our family. ☐

Today I scored ☐ out of 6.

Week 8 — Day 2

Rewrite the sentences below, adding capital letters in the correct places.

hugo read with layla today.

Hugo read with Layla today.

(1) we played games on thursday.

....

(2) grace and i painted pictures.

....

(3) dan and lee watch insects.

....

(4) he writes stories with jameela.

....

Today I scored [ ] out of 8.

Year 1 English — Summer Term

Week 8 — Day 3

Read each sentence, then circle the correct spelling of the word in bold.

1 We made scarecro**w**s **today** / **todai**.

2 That one has **blue** / **blew** cloth**e**s.

3 The crows **a**ll **flew** / **floo** away.

4 We made he**r** out of **stror** / **straw**.

5 **Which** / **Wich** one do you like best?

6 Ca**n** I **joyn** / **join** in and make one?

7 I **g**ot some cloth for his **trowsers** / **trousers**.

8 The green letters spell out a word.
Write the word to complete the sentence.

He is .... a green coat.

Today I scored ☐ out of 8.

Week 8 — Day 4

Write the words in the correct order to make a sentence. Remember to add the punctuation mark in the correct place.

have | blue | I | a | skateboard | .

I have a blue skateboard.

1 tricks | she | Can | do | ? | some

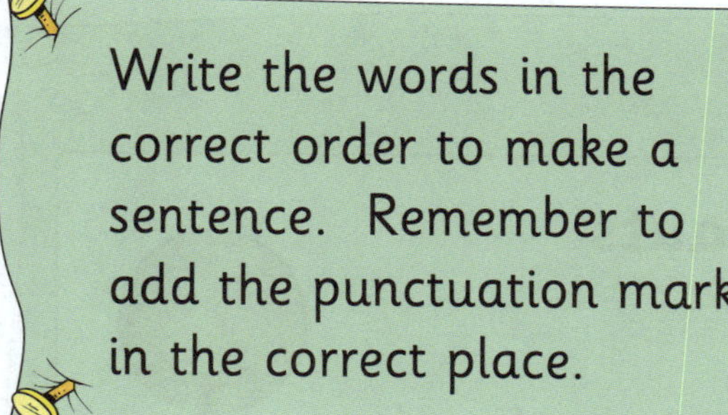

....

2 he | high | ! | how | is | Look

....

3 green | . | He | helmet | wears | his

....

4 go | How | ? | fast | you | can

....

Today I scored [ ] out of 4.

Year 1 English — Summer Term

Week 8 — Day 5

Read the text, then answer the questions.

Facts About Astronauts

- Astronauts travel through space.
- Their rockets can fly in **cercles** around the Earth.
- They take pictures of other planets to learn about them.
- They live in a space station until it is time to return home.

1 Where do astronauts travel?

....

2 Write the correct spelling of the word in bold.

cercles   ....

3 What do astronauts need to help them learn about planets?

a radio ☐   a camera ☐   a diary ☐

4 According to the text, when do astronauts leave the space station?

....

Today I scored ☐ out of 4.

Week 9 — Day 1

Read each sentence, then circle the word in bold that is spelt correctly.

We went for a walk **tonight** / **tonyt**.

1 There were clouds in the **ski** / **sky**.

2 The moon was very **brite** / **bright**.

3 The **light** / **lyt** helped us to see.

4 We walked on the sand **by** / **bie** the sea.

5 I saw a dolphin jump and **dive** / **dyve**.

6 I had to stop and **tigh** / **tie** my laces.

7 There was a **pile** / **pyl** of lovely shells.

8 I **mite** / **might** take some shells home.

Today I scored ☐ out of 8.

Year 1 English — Summer Term

Week 9 — Day 2

Read each sentence, then circle the letters missing from the word in bold.

I __**ck** a ball in the park.   ci   (ki)

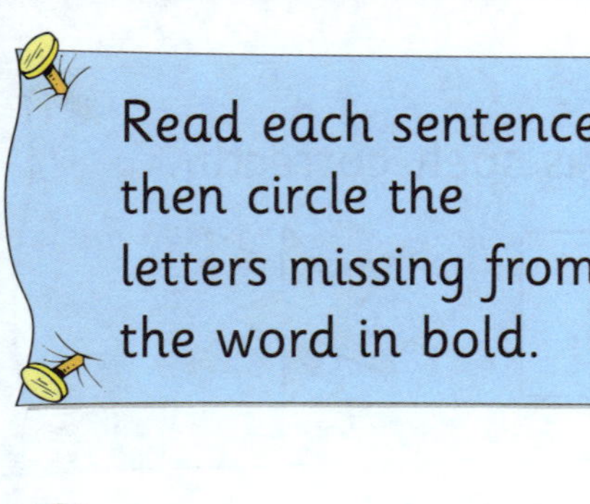

1 The **s__** is very blue today.   cy   ky

2 Mum puts sun cream on my **s__n**.   ki   ci

3 I can read my __**mics**.   ko   co

4 I m__**e** lots of new friends.   ack   ak

5 Dad takes photos with a __**mera**.   ca   ka

6 A ladybird __**awled** on my hand.   kr   cr

7 Lily flies her new __**te**.   ki   ci

8 We found a se__**et** den.   cr   kr

Today I scored ____ out of 8.

Week 9 — Day 3

Use the words in the boxes to complete the sentences. You should only use each word once.

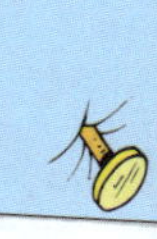

We ...should... have a tea party.

special   share   Charlotte

sure   options   sugar

1   Liam and Ed will .... some chocolate cake.

2   There are lots of drink ....

3   We should use the .... cups.

4   Nico said he did not want ....

5   Are you .... you want more tea?

6   .... eats a pink cupcake.

Today I scored ☐ out of 6.

Year 1 English — Summer Term

Week 9 — Day 4

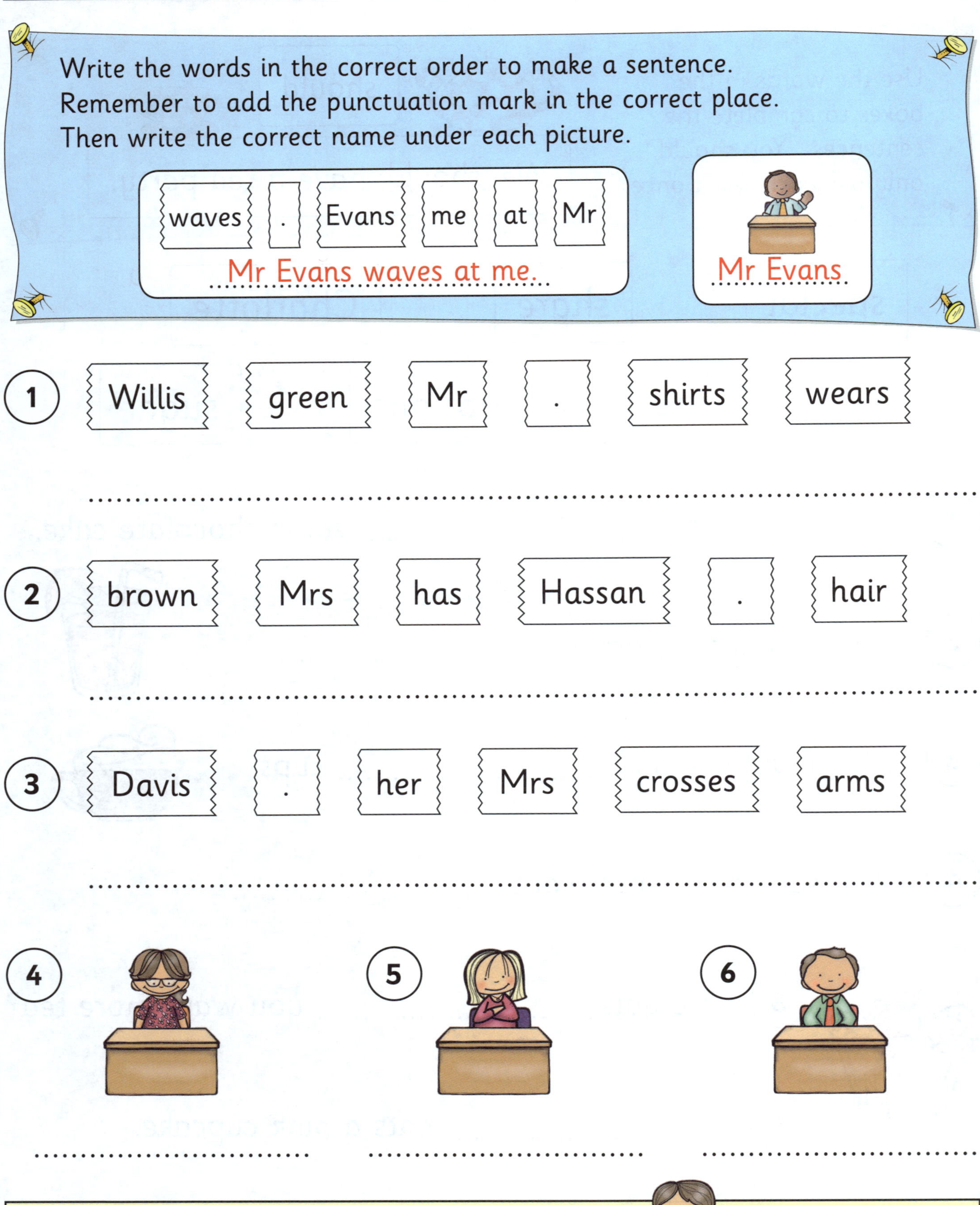

Write the words in the correct order to make a sentence.
Remember to add the punctuation mark in the correct place.
Then write the correct name under each picture.

1. Willis green Mr . shirts wears

2. brown Mrs has Hassan . hair

3. Davis . her Mrs crosses arms

4.   5.   6.

Today I scored ☐ out of 6.

Week 9 — Day 5

Read the text, then answer the questions.

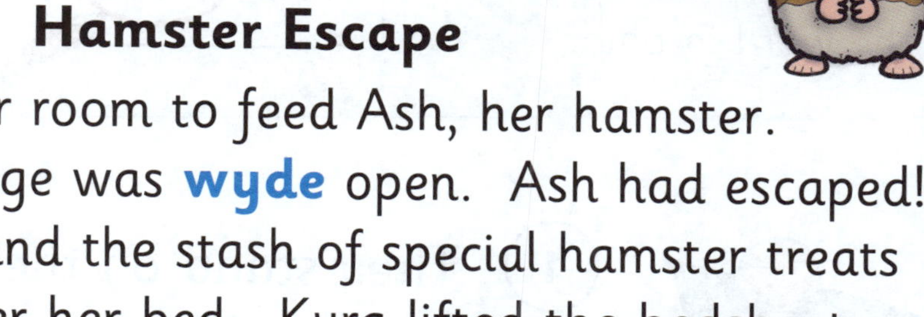

Hamster Escape

Kyra went into her room to feed Ash, her hamster. The door of his cage was **wyde** open. Ash had escaped! Maybe he had found the stash of special hamster treats that she kept under her bed. Kyra lifted the bedsheet and saw him nibbling on the treats. Phew, he was safe!

1   Write the correct spelling of the word in bold.

wyde ....

2   Why does Kyra go into her room?

....

3   Where does Kyra find her hamster?

under her bed ☐   under her desk ☐   outside ☐

4   Rewrite this sentence so that it makes sense.
'Kyra put Ash his cage in.'

....

Today I scored ☐ out of 4.

    Year 1 English — Summer Term

Week 10 — Day 1

Read each sentence, then circle the correct spelling of the word in bold.

1 They stand on the **leaf** / **leef**.

2 One lands on a **peece** / **piece** of fruit.

3 **Thees** / **These** bees live in my garden.

4 Is their hive **emptie** / **empty**?

5 That one is the **quean** / **queen**.

6 The bees work as a **team** / **tiem**.

7 The honey they make is **sweet** / **swete**.

8 She visits them **everie** / **every** week.

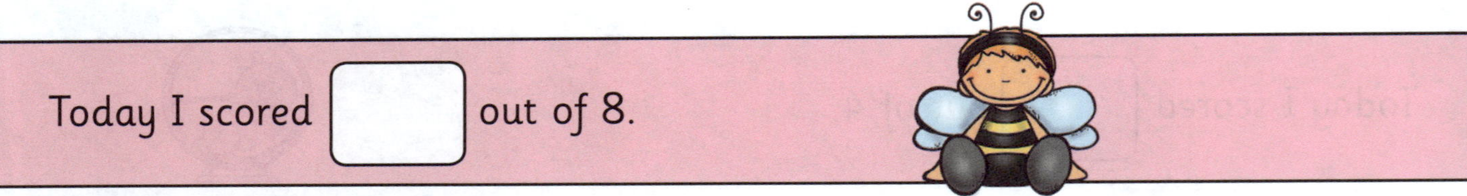

Today I scored ☐ out of 8.

Week 10 — Day 2

Write the words in the correct order to make a sentence. Add a full stop or a question mark to the end of each sentence.

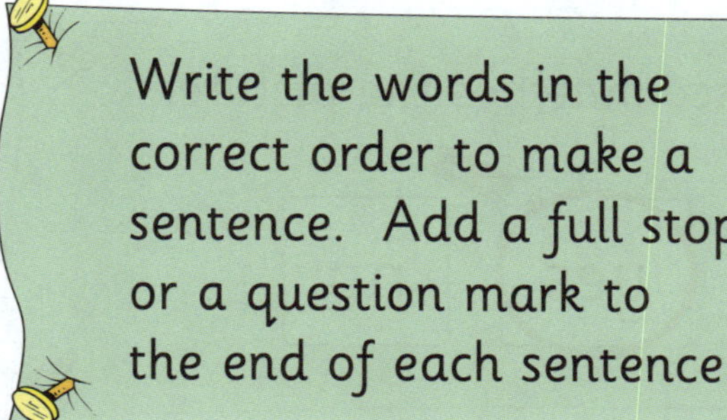

The hill looked very tall.

1. 

....

2. will up me Who pull

....

3. 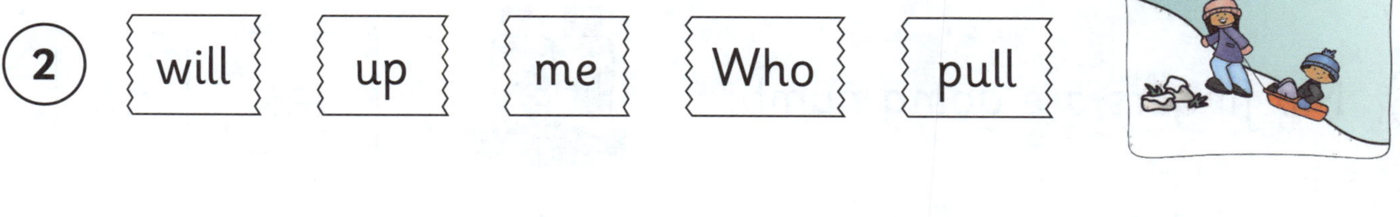

....

4. fallen Have yet you off

....

Today I scored ☐ out of 8.

     Year 1 English — Summer Term

Week 10 — Day 3

Circle 'yes' or 'no' to show whether each sentence matches the picture.

The lamb has escaped.  yes no

1. The plumber left the door open.  yes no

2. There is a trail of crumbs.  yes no

3. My fingers are going numb.  yes no

4. She climbed onto the roof.  yes no

5. The comb is stuck in her wool.  yes no

6. Oh no, she bit my thumb!  yes no

7. She has hurt one of her limbs.  yes no

Today I scored [ ] out of 7. 

Week 10 — Day 4

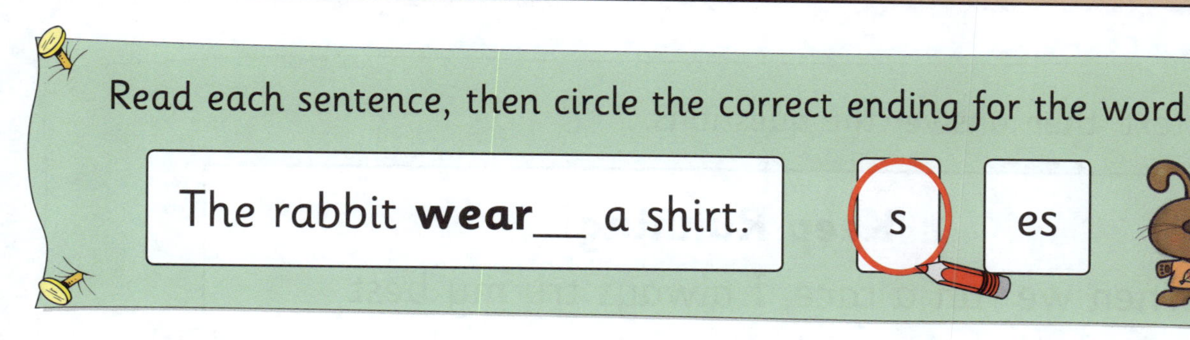

Read each sentence, then circle the correct ending for the word in bold.

The rabbit **wear**__ a shirt.   s   es

1. The rabbit **chew**__ a carrot.   ed   ing

2. It **hold**__ a yellow flower.   s   es

3. She **play**__ with a stick.   ed   ing

4. The rabbit **stretch**__ the string.   s   es

5. He likes **rest**__ on toadstools.   ing   es

6. She **crunch**__ the apples in her mouth.   s   es

7. He **pull**__ the wagon full of leaves.   ing   ed

Today I scored [ ] out of 7.

     Year 1 English — Summer Term

Week 10 — Day 5

Read the text, then answer the questions.

Keep Running!

When we run a race, I always try my best to beat Kai. He is the fastest in our class, so he always wins. I doubt I will ever **reech** the finish line before him, but I am going to try. I just need to practise running at home.

1 Write the correct spelling of the word in bold.

reech ....

2 What do the children do together?

....

3 Why does Kai always win?

He cheats. ☐   He is fast. ☐   He likes running. ☐

4 What can the storyteller do to beat Kai?

....

Today I scored ☐ out of 4.

Week 11 — Day 1

Read each sentence, then circle the word in bold that is spelt correctly.

They are **heroes** / **herows**.

(1) A thief **stoal** / **stole** my new spade.

(2) I saw him through the **window** / **windo**.

(3) The penguins **folload** / **followed** the thief.

(4) I **hoaped** / **hoped** they would catch him.

(5) The thief went down a short **road** / **rode**.

(6) The penguins saw him **beloe** / **below** them.

(7) He **groened** / **groaned** when he got trapped.

(8) He was too slow for **those** / **thoas** penguins.

Today I scored [ ] out of 8.

Year 1 English — Summer Term

Week 11 — Day 2

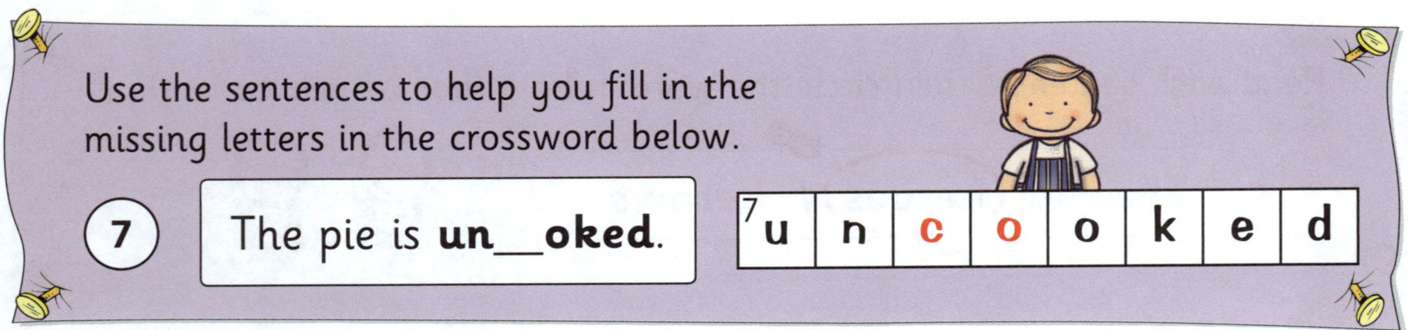

Use the sentences to help you fill in the missing letters in the crossword below.

7 The pie is **un__oked**.

| ⁷u | n | c | o | o | k | e | d |

1 We were **un__re** what to do next.

2 Freddie **unwr__ped** a block of butter.

3 We put away the **unu__d** eggs.

4 Auntie Becky put the **un__ked** pie in the oven.

5 I **unc__ped** the can of squirty cream.

6 I helped clean up the **un___dy** kitchen.

Week 11 — Day 3

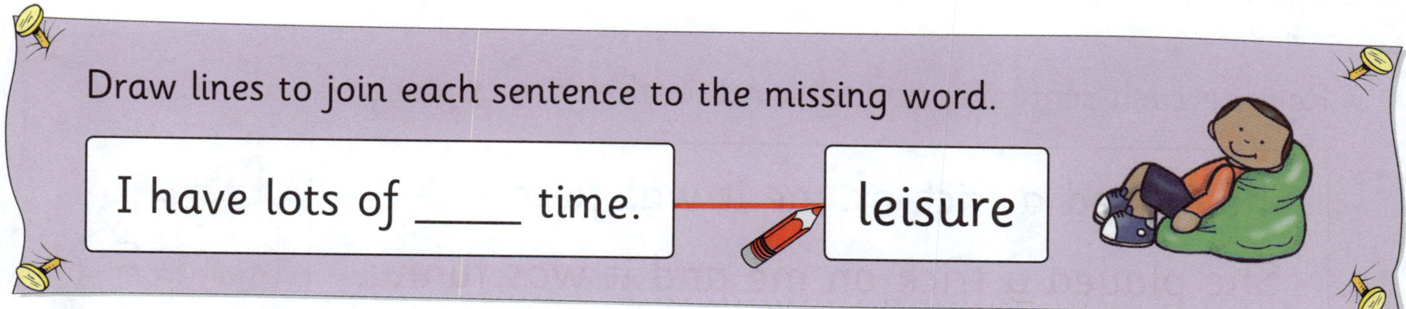

Draw lines to join each sentence to the missing word.

I have lots of _____ time. — leisure

(1) We bought a new _____.

usually

(2) I _____ watch a pirate show.

treasures

(3) Where are the _____?

television

(4) They make a _____ about where to go.

unusual

(5) They _____ their gold.

decision

(6) The pirates have an _____ parrot.

measured

Today I scored [ ] out of 6.

Year 1 English — Summer Term

Week 11 — Day 4

Rewrite each sentence, adding '**and**' in the correct place.

> She played a trick on me it was funny.
>
> She played a trick on me and it was funny.

1 She jumped out of a pile of pillows blankets.

....

....

2 There was a fake spider it made me jump.

....

....

3 I opened the box a balloon floated out.

....

....

Today I scored [ ] out of 3.

Week 11 — Day 5

Read the text, then answer the questions.

How to Grow Your Own Alien

1. Fill a bowl with space dust and make a hole in the middle.
2. Put a magic stone inside and sprinkle moon water over it.
3. Put the bowl under a window in your home.
4. When the stone goes blue, the alien is ready.
5. When it hatches, **shoa** all of your friends!

1 Write the correct spelling of the word in bold.

shoa ....

2 What do you need to put in the hole?

an alien seed ☐   a magic stone ☐   star powder ☐

3 Where should you put the bowl?

....

4 What happens when the alien is ready to hatch?

....

Today I scored ☐ out of 4.

Year 1 English — Summer Term

Week 12 — Day 1

Read each sentence, then circle the correct spelling of the word in bold.

1 I moved to this street last **year** / **yeer**.

2 Sue **steared** / **steered** her bike carefully.

3 Milo has a **fere** / **fear** of insects.

4 Kate plays with her fluffy **dere** / **deer**.

5 Bring the ball over **here** / **hear**.

6 It is **clear** / **cleer** that Jay is scared of robots.

7 We **heer** / **hear** the ice cream van.

8 We **cheer** / **chere** and run towards it.

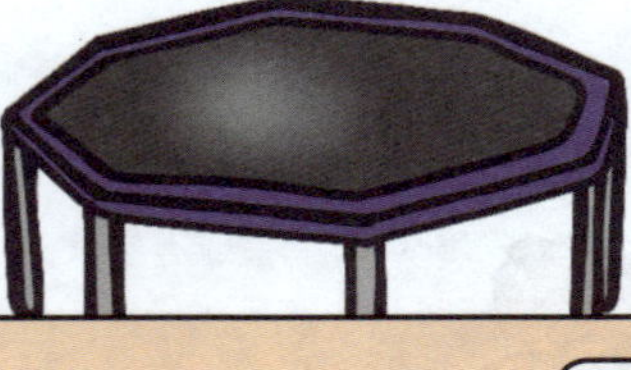

Today I scored ☐ out of 8.

Week 12 — Day 2

Rewrite each sentence, making sure you put a capital letter in the correct place. Add either an exclamation mark or a question mark to finish each sentence.

what a fun trip

What a fun trip!

1 what a good photo

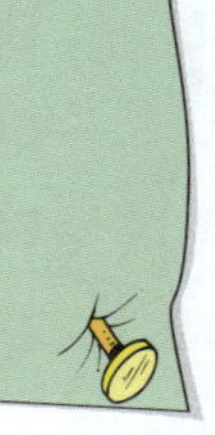

....

2 where is the castle

....

3 how amazing it looks

....

4 holidays are so much fun

....

5 when does the tour start

....

Today I scored ☐ out of 10.

Year 1 English — Summer Term

Week 12 — Day 3

Read each sentence, then circle the correct spelling of the word in the box.

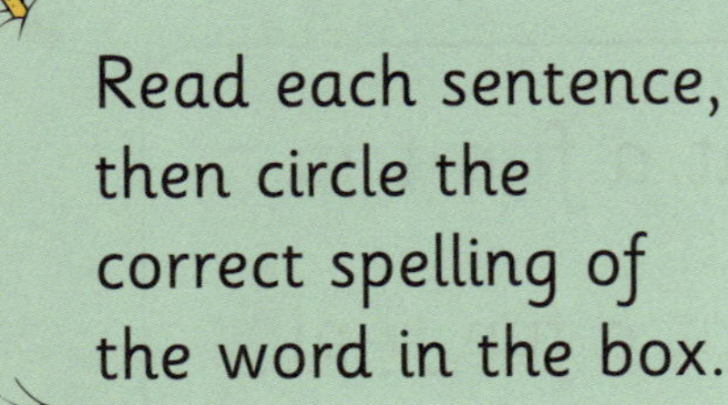

1 She went past a hurd herd of cows.

2 I like the colour colur of his scooter.

3 Avi got his new scooter on Thursday Thersday .

4 Eve almost crashed into the kurb kerb .

5 Ted had to swurve swerve to miss the bin.

6 She fell off and hurt hert her knee.

Today I scored ⬜ out of 6.

Week 12 — Day 4

Look at the pictures, then read the sentences. Use the numbers 1 to 4 to put the sentences in the right order. Write a sentence on the line to describe the final picture.

1) The spider put a hat on and did a little dance. ☐

2) I felt tired so I went upstairs to my room. ☐

3) I was surprised to see the spider and I screamed. ☐

4) A spider was sitting in the middle of my bed. ☐

5) 5

Today I scored ☐ out of 5.

Year 1 English — Summer Term

Week 12 — Day 5

Read the text, then answer the questions.

> Anna volunteered to help her mum in the garden. It was cold, so she wore a hat to keep her ears warm. Anna planted some turnips and then she picked some **hurbs** to put in their dinner. After a while, her dad came out with some hot drinks. Anna smiled and ran over to him.

(1) Write the correct spelling of the word in bold.

hurbs ....

(2) What is the weather like in the garden? Tick one box.

wet ☐   warm ☐   cold ☐

(3) Who else is working in the garden?

....

(4) How does Anna feel when her dad brings her a hot drink? Circle one word.

worried   bored   pleased

Today I scored ☐ out of 4.

Answers

Week 1 — Day 1

1. He is the winner.
2. I like running races.
3. Ben ran very fast.
4. Oti has a medal.
   (For each question, 1 mark for correctly reordering the words and 1 mark for adding a full stop in the correct place.)

Week 1 — Day 2

1. I **dive** into the sea.
2. He surfed a big **wave**.
3. They **love** the water.
4. I **have** so much fun.
5. She saw **five** fish.
6. Mum **gave** me a lolly.

Week 1 — Day 3

1. I had a party. All my friends were there.
   (1 mark for each full stop)
2. We all wore fancy dress. Everyone looked good.
   (1 mark for each full stop)
3. I wore my monster costume. It is blue.
   (1 mark for each full stop)
4. Tia came as a bee. She loves insects.
   (1 mark for each full stop)
5. Dad made a cake. He put candles on top.
   (1 mark for each full stop)
6. We played games. Pass the parcel is the best.
   (1 mark for each full stop)

Week 1 — Day 4

1. Will you **do** a dance with me?
2. I can show you what to **do**.
3. First take **one** big jump forward.
4. Then do a **little** hop to the right.
5. March on the spot a **little** bit.
6. Kick **one** of your legs in the air.
7. Now **do** it all again!

Week 1 — Day 5

1. a list
2. one
3. camping
4. 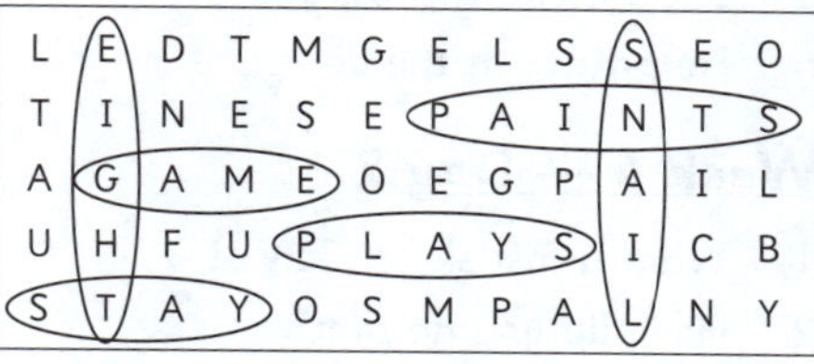

Week 2 — Day 1

1. Bella is **proud** of her plant.
2. **How** many leaves does it have?
3. Nigel plants seeds in the **ground**.
4. The mud is **brown** and sticky.
5. Emma **found** a huge leaf.
6. She is **allowed** to keep it.
7. Eric put his arms **around** the tree.
8. The tree **towers** over him.

Week 2 — Day 2

1. Her cat is grey **and** yours is black.
2. My cat was playing **and** she got wet.
3. Tiger was tired **and** he fell asleep.

Week 2 — Day 3

1. The zebra **wriggles** when I tickle it.
2. The sloth will **rest** on the branch.
3. The toucan sat on his **wrist.**
4. The rhino has **wrinkly** skin.
5. The hippo has **rolled** in the mud.
6. The baby bears enjoy **wrestling** each other.
7. The giraffe is **ready** for her lunch.

Week 2 — Day 4

1. Last week, **i** read five books.
2. Fen's book is set in **bristol**.
3. The best writer is **amy** Peterson.
4. Malia and I like books about **japan**.
5. I want to be a writer when **i** am older.
6. We go to the library every **friday**.
7. **my** sister likes reading about lorries.

Week 2 — Day 5

1. 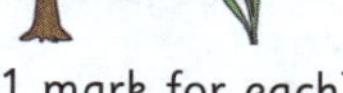
   (1 mark for each)
2. April
3. showers
4. raindrops

Week 3 — Day 1

L	E	D	T	M	G	E	L	S	S	E	O
T	I	N	E	S	E	P	A	I	N	T	S
A	G	A	M	E	O	E	G	P	A	I	L
U	H	F	U	P	L	A	Y	S	I	C	B
S	T	A	Y	O	S	M	P	A	L	N	Y

Week 3 — Day 2

1. Who are you**?**
2. You are very tall.
3. Shall we be friends**?**
4. How far can you fly**?**
5. He is my dad.
6. You have a long tail.
7. The egg is spotty.
8. Are you hungry**?**
9. Do you like cookies**?**
10. Where is she going**?**

Week 3 — Day 3

1. no
2. yes
3. yes
4. no
5. yes
6. no
7. no
8. yes

Week 3 — Day 4

1. My grandma is **older** than my grandpa.
2. You have the **longest** hair of all.
3. I am **taller** than my sisters.
4. He has the **loudest** voice out of us.
5. Nick is the **fastest** in our class.
6. My brother is **younger** than me.
7. Kelvin is **shorter** than Mia.
8. Dev is the **cleverest** out of everyone.

Week 3 — Day 5

1. tails
2. jumping
3. porridge and jelly
   (1 mark for each)
4. One mark for a drawing of a
   badger, a snail or some jam.

Week 4 — Day 1

1. Do not **spoil** the surprise.
2. I hear the puppy make a **noise**.
3. The puppy **joined** our family.
4. I will buy her some dog **toys**.
5. She will not **annoy** you.
6. He **points** at the door.

Week 4 — Day 2

1. What a fast skater Jon is**!**
2. How did you do that**?**
3. He is standing on one leg**!**
4. Can they do lots of tricks**?**
5. Why did that girl fall over**?**
6. How cosy your scarf looks**!**
7. Do you think he is the best skater**?**
8. Skating with my sister is fun**!**

Week 4 — Day 3

1. You can win lots of di**ff**erent things.
2. Bilal won some flu**ff**y earmuffs.
3. This teddy is so so**f**t.
4. Fred just won a **f**ancy pen.
5. I cuddled my new ele**ph**ant toy.
6. I wanted to win the box of to**ff**ees.
7. Can you take a **ph**oto of
   me with my prize?

Week 4 — Day 4

1. He searches in the trees**.**
2. He looks behind the flowers**.**
3. There are none up here**.**
4. He finds lots of acorns**.**
   (For each question, 1 mark for
   correctly reordering the words and
   1 mark for adding a full stop in the
   correct place.)

Week 4 — Day 5

1. choice
2. a ladder
3. watched her
4. 

Week 5 — Day 1

1. Mum does m**ore** writing than me.
2. I s**aw** her books in the shop.
3. I like writing st**or**ies too.
4. I write them f**or** my sister.
5. My new story is about a h**au**nted
   house.
6. Spooky creatures c**au**se trouble.
7. I will dr**aw** a picture of it.

Week 5 — Day 2

1. Stop making such a mess!
2. You can weigh out the flour.
3. We need to find a big cake tin.
4. Do not touch the oven!
5. Now we add the strawberry icing.
6. What a large and fancy cake!

Week 5 — Day 3

1. It is **nice** to walk around.
2. I have been here **twice** before.
3. Where is the **science** fair?
4. It was hard to find parking **spaces**.
5. People work in those **offices**.
6. We **forced** our way through the
   crowd.
7. I saw a film at that **cinema**.

Week 5 — Day 4

1. lunch**b**ox
2. whit**e**board
3. cl**a**ssroom
4. pla**y**groun**d**
5. work**s**he**e**t
6. I like to play o**uts**id**e**.

Week 5 — Day 5

1. a goose
2. born
3. He grew a lot.
4. They will need a new barn door.

Week 6 — Day 1

1. The **crew** are on their way.
2. They rescued a cat from the **roof**.
3. They flashed their **blue** lights.
4. I want to be a firefighter **too**.
5. I heard the sirens from my **room**.
6. The policewoman looked for a stolen
   flute.
7. He **flew** over in a helicopter.
8. It is **true** that they are heroes.

Week 6 — Day 2

1. She asks him questions.
2. What did she say?
3. He holds the camera.
4. Is the weather nice?

Week 6 — Day 3

1. She **watches** the weather carefully.
2. **Which** way is the ship sailing?
3. A light is coming from the **window**.
4. The captain turns the
   wheel to steer the ship.
5. It is **windy** at the top of the
   lighthouse.
6. Sometimes, Ella sees a
   whale in the sea.

Week 6 — Day 4

1. Haruki and Jack found two skull**s**.
2. My camera is in one of the box**es**.
3. Those dinosaurs had large head**s**!
4. She brush**es** all of the soil away.
5. Raina put**s** the small bones in jars.
6. Finn touch**es** the broken pieces.
7. Alice want**s** to find an old tooth.
8. Gino digs near the bush**es**.

Week 6 — Day 5

1. include
2. rescue people
   watch the pool
   (1 mark for each)
3. in case they slip / so they don't slip
4. He blew his silver whistle.

Week 7 — Day 1

1. Karl has a **spare** sheet of paper.
2. Abby sits on her **chair**.
3. Stephen likes to **wear** warm hats.
4. Kayla has a **pair** of red boots.
5. Tom **stares** at the cake.
6. India has her foot in the **air**.
7. Eric always **shares** his presents.
8. Clara has gone to the **fair**.

Week 7 — Day 2

1. Can you reach the top of the tree**?**
2. I am holding on as tight as I can.
3. Shelly is hanging upside down.
4. How did you get up there so fast**?**
5. There is a very good view from the top.
6. Are your arms feeling tired yet**?**
7. Which tree shall we go up next**?**
8. I will sit on this branch for a rest.

Week 7 — Day 3

1. The stick helps her sore **knee**.
2. I **need** to visit my grandparents.
3. Grandma got me a toy **knight**.
4. Grandad gave his dog a bone to **gnaw**.
5. We went to the **nearby** shops.
6. Grandad taught me to tie **knots**.
7. There are **gnomes** in their garden.

Week 7 — Day 4

1. Have you seen my ribbon**?**
2. Tim bought a green top.
3. Why is your jumper dirty**?**
4. Her top has white dots.

Week 7 — Day 5

1. 
2. brown
3. scared
4. the branch (knocking against the window)

Week 8 — Day 1

1. Her **birthday** is in October.
2. The **nurse** brings the baby a blanket.
3. The blanket is soft and **purple**.
4. She wakes up **early** in the morning.
5. Do not **disturb** her when she is sleeping.
6. She is the **third** child in our family.

Week 8 — Day 2

1. **W**e played games on **T**hursday. (1 mark for each)
2. **G**race and **I** painted pictures. (1 mark for each)
3. **D**an and **L**ee watch insects. (1 mark for each)
4. **H**e writes stories with **J**ameela. (1 mark for each)

Week 8 — Day 3

1. We made scarecrows **today**.
2. That one has **blue** clothes.
3. The crows all **flew** away.
4. We made her out of **straw**.
5. **Which** one do you like best?
6. Can I **join** in and make one?
7. I got some cloth for his **trousers**.
8. He is **wearing** a green coat.

Week 8 — Day 4

1. Can she do some tricks?
2. Look how high he is!
3. He wears his green helmet.
4. How fast can you go?

Week 8 — Day 5

1. through space
2. circles
3. a camera
4. when it is time to return home

Week 9 — Day 1

1. There were clouds in the **sky**.
2. The moon was very **bright**.
3. The **light** helped us to see.
4. We walked on the sand **by** the sea.
5. I saw a dolphin jump and **dive**.
6. I had to stop and **tie** my laces.
7. There was a **pile** of lovely shells.
8. I **might** take some shells home.

Week 9 — Day 2

1. The s**ky** is very blue today.
2. Mum puts sun cream on my s**kin**.
3. I can read my **co**mics.
4. I m**ake** lots of new friends.
5. Dad takes photos with a **ca**mera.
6. A ladybird **cr**awled on my hand.
7. Lily flies her new **ki**te.
8. We found a se**cr**et den.

Week 9 — Day 3

1. Liam and Ed will **share** some chocolate cake.
2. There are lots of drink **options**.
3. We should use the **special** cups.
4. Nico said he did not want **sugar**.
5. Are you **sure** you want more tea?
6. **Charlotte** eats a pink cupcake.

Week 9 — Day 4

1. Mr Willis wears green shirts.
2. Mrs Hassan has brown hair.
3. Mrs Davis crosses her arms.
4. Mrs Hassan
5. Mrs Davis
6. Mr Willis

Week 9 — Day 5

1. wide
2. to feed her hamster
3. under her bed
4. Kyra put Ash in his cage.

Week 10 — Day 1

1. They stand on the **leaf**.
2. One lands on a **piece** of fruit.
3. **These** bees live in my garden.
4. Is their hive **empty**?
5. That one is the **queen**.
6. The bees work as a **team**.
7. The honey they make is **sweet**.
8. She visits them **every** week.

Week 10 — Day 2

1. Watch me slide down here.
2. Who will pull me up**?**
3. She called out to us.
4. Have you fallen off yet**?** (For each question, 1 mark for correctly reordering the words and 1 mark for adding the correct punctuation mark.)

Week 10 — Day 3

1. yes
2. no
3. no
4. yes
5. yes
6. no
7. yes

Week 10 — Day 4

1. The rabbit chew**ed** a carrot.
2. It hold**s** a yellow flower.
3. She play**ed** with a stick.
4. The rabbit stretch**es** the string.
5. He likes rest**ing** on toadstools.
6. She crunch**es** the apples in her mouth.
7. He pull**ed** the wagon full of leaves.

Answers

Week 10 — Day 5

1. reach
2. They run a race.
3. He is fast.
4. They can practise running at home.

Week 11 — Day 1

1. A thief **stole** my new spade.
2. I saw him through the **window**.
3. The penguins **followed** the thief.
4. I **hoped** they would catch him.
5. The thief went down a short **road**.
6. The penguins saw him **below** them.
7. He **groaned** when he got trapped.
8. He was too slow for **those** penguins.

Week 11 — Day 2

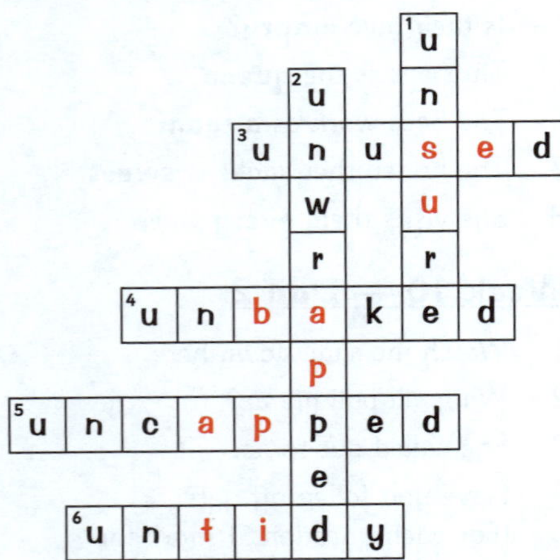

Week 11 — Day 3

1. We bought a new **television**.
2. I **usually** watch a pirate show.
3. Where are the **treasures**?
4. They make a **decision** about where to go.
5. They **measured** their gold
6. The pirates have an **unusual** parrot.

Week 11 — Day 4

1. She jumped out of a pile of pillows **and** blankets.
2. There was a fake spider **and** it made me jump.
3. I opened the box **and** a balloon floated out.

Week 11 — Day 5

1. show
2. a magic stone
3. under a window (in your home)
4. The stone goes blue.

Week 12 — Day 1

1. I moved to this street last **year**.
2. Sue **steered** her bike carefully.
3. Milo has a **fear** of insects.
4. Kate plays with her fluffy **deer**.
5. Bring the ball over **here**.
6. It is **clear** that Jay is scared of robots.
7. We **hear** the ice cream van.
8. We **cheer** and run towards it.

Week 12 — Day 2

1. **W**hat a good photo!
   (1 mark for each)
2. **W**here is the castle**?**
   (1 mark for each)
3. **H**ow amazing it looks!
   (1 mark for each)
4. **H**olidays are so much fun!
   (1 mark for each)
5. **W**hen does the tour start**?**
   (1 mark for each)

Week 12 — Day 3

1. She went past a **herd** of cows.
2. I like the **colour** of his scooter.
3. Avi got his new scooter on **Thursday**.
4. Eve almost crashed into the **kerb**.
5. Ted had to **swerve** to miss the bin.
6. She fell off and **hurt** her knee.

Week 12 — Day 4

1. The spider put a hat on and did a little dance. — 4
2. I felt tired so I went upstairs to my room. — 1
3. I was surprised to see the spider and I screamed. — 3
4. A spider was sitting in the middle of my bed. — 2
5. E.g. I laughed at the spider.

Week 12 — Day 5

1. herbs
2. cold
3. Anna's mum
4. pleased